Edmund B. O'Callaghan

Papers Relating to the First Settlement of New York by the Dutch

Containing a list of the early immigrants to New Netherland, 1657-1664

Edmund B. O'Callaghan

Papers Relating to the First Settlement of New York by the Dutch
Containing a list of the early immigrants to New Netherland, 1657-1664

ISBN/EAN: 9783337309510

Printed in Europe, USA, Canada, Australia, Japan

Cover: Foto ©Suzi / pixelio.de

More available books at **www.hansebooks.com**

[COLLECTANEA ADAMANTÆA. XXVII.]

PAPERS RELATING TO

THE

First Settlement of New York

BY THE DUTCH,

CONTAINING

A LIST OF THE EARLY IMMIGRANTS TO NEW NETHERLAND;

1657-1664.

From the " Documentary History of New York,"

AND

The Description and First Settlement of New Netherland,

From " Wassenaer's Historie van Europa."

IN TWO VOLUMES.
VOL. I.

PRIVATELY PRINTED.
EDINBURGH.
1888.

List of Early Immigrants
to
New Netherlands.

Early Immigrants

TO

New Netherland;

1657-1664.

1657.

April; *In the Draetvat.*

Arent Janssen ; house carpenter, and wife and daughter.

Marcus de Chousoy, and wife, two workmen, and two boys.

Teunis Craey, from Venlo, and wife and four children and two servants.

Heinrich Stoeff.

Jacob Hendricksen Haen ; painter.

Adriaen Vincent.

Johannis Smetdes.
Dirk Buyskes.

December; *In the Gilded Otter.*

Claes Pouwelson from Detmarsum ; mason.
Jan Jansen van den Bos ; mason, and his brother.

Ditto ; *In the Jan Baptiste.*

Jan Sudeich, and wife and two children.
Claes Sudeich.
Adam Breemen, from Aecken.
Douwe Claessen from Medemblick ; mason.
Cornelis Barentsen Vande Kuyl.
Thys Jacobsen.

1658.

MAY; *In the Moesman.*

Jan Adriaensen van Duyvelant.
Christina Bleyers from Stoltenau.
Ursel Dircks from Holstein, and two children.
Geertzen Buyers.

DITTO; *In the Gilded Beaver.*

Jan Barentsen house carpenter, and workman.
Anthony de Mis from Haerlem, and wife and two children.
The wife of Andries vander Sluys; Clerk in Fort Orange, and child.
Charel Fonteyn; a Frenchman, and wife.
Peter Claessen, from Holstein; farmer and wife and two children.
Gerrit Gerritsen van Gilthuys; taylor.
Jan Jansen; house carpenter, and wife and four children.
Jan Gouwenberch, from Hoorn.
Adriaen van Laer, from Amsterdam, and servant.
Jan Gerretsen Buytenhuys; baker, and wife, and sucking child.

Willem van Vredenburch.

Cornelis Andriessen Hoogland ; taylor.

Peter van Halen, from Utrecht, and wife, two children, and boy.

Simon Bouché.

Cornelis Hendricksen van Ens.

Jan Evertsen van Gloockens.

Tryntje Pieters ; maiden.

JUNE; *In the Brownfish.*

Jannetje Volckertse wife of Evert Luykese; baker, and daughter.

Douwe Harmsen, from Friesland, and wife and four children.

Adriaen Jansen, from Zea-land; fisherman.

Francois Abrahamsen, from Flissingen.

Joris Jansen, from Hoorn ; house carpenter.

Jan Aerensen van Kampen; farmer.

Jan Isbrands; rope maker.

Huybert de Bruyn.

Machteld Stoffelsen ; widow, is acquainted with agriculture.

Dirck Smith, Ensign in the Company's service,* and a sucking child.

---

*Served in the Esopus war with great credit ; he died Anno 1660 to the regret of the Director General and council. His widow thereupon returned to Holland.

Jannetje Hermens; maiden, and her brother Jan Harmensen.

Maria Claes; maiden.

Francisco de Gordosa from Davingen.

Charles Garet.

Jan Leynie, from Paris.

Dorigeman Jansen, from Dordrecht and his bride.

Claes Wolf, from the Elbe ; sailor.

Harmen Dircksen from Norway and wife and child.

Adam van Santen, and wife and two children.

1659.

February; *In the Faith.*

Jan Woutersen, from Ravesteyn ; shoemaker, and wife and daughter.

Catalyntje Cranenburg ; maiden.

Jan van Coppenol, from Remsen ; farmer, and wife and two children.

Matthys Roelofs, from Denmark, and wife and child.

Sophia Roeloffs.

Geertruy Jochems, from Hamburgh ; wife of Claes Claessen from Amersfoot, now in N. Netherland ; and two children.

Peter Corneliss, from Holsteyn ; labourer.

Peter Jacobs, from Holsteyn.

Josyntje Verhagen, from Middleburg, and daughter.

Saertge Hendricks, from Delft.

Egbert Meynderts, from Amsterdam, and wife and child and servant.

Jan Leurens Noorman and wife.

Harmen Coerten, from Voorhuysen, and wife and five children.

Magalantje Teunis, from Voorhuysen.

Feytje Dircks.

Gillis Jansen van Garder, and wife and four children.

Bastiaen Clement, from Doornick.

Adriaen Fournoi, from Valenciennes.

Jannetje Eyckers, from East Friesland.

Joris Jorissen Townsen, from Redfort ; mason.

Nicholas Gillissen Marschal.

Wouter Gerritsen van Kootuyck.

Jan Jacobsen, from Utrecht ; farmer, and wife, mother and two children.

Arent Francken van Iperen.

Dennys Isacksen, from Wyck by Daurstede.

Weyntje Martens van Gorehem.

Vroutje Gerrits, wife of Cosyn Gerritsen; wheelwright.

Jan Dircksen, from Alckmaer, and wife and three children.

Nettert Jansen, from Embden.

Epke Jacobs, from Harlingen ; farmer, and wife and five sons.

Stoffiel Gerritsen from Laer.

Jan Meynderts, from Iperen; farmer, and wife.

Jan Barents Ameshof, from Amsterdam.

Symon Drune from Henegouw.

Hendrick Harmensen, from Amsterdam.

Evert Cornellissen, from the vicinity of Amersfoort.

Laurens Jacobs van der Wielen.

Jannetje Theunis van Ysselstein.

Jan Roelofsen, van Naerden ; farmer.

Jacob Hendricks, from the Highland, and maid servant.

Goossen van Twiller, from New-Kerk.

Lawrens Janssen, from Wormer.

Jan Harmens, from Amersfoort; taylor, and wife and four children.

Evert Marschal; glasier, from Amsterdam and wife and daughter.

Boele Roelofsen, Joncker, and wife and four children, besides his wife's sister and a boy.

DITTO; *In the Otter.*

Carel Bevois, from Leyden; and wife and three children.

Martin Warnarts Stolten, from Swoll.

Cornelis Jansen vander veer; farmer.

Jan Luycas, from Oldenseel; shoemaker, and wife and suckling.

Roelof Dircksen, from Sweden.

Sweris Dirxsz, from Sweden.

APRIL; *In the Beaver.*

Peter Arentsen Diesvelt; taylor.

Amadeas Fougie, Frenchman, farmer.

Jacques Reneau, Frenchman; agriculturer.

Jacques Monier, Frenchman ; agriculturer.

Pierre Monier, Frenchman ; agriculturer.

Matthieu Savariau, Frenchman ; agriculturer.

Pierre Grissaut, Frenchman; agriculturist.

Maintien Jans, from Amsterdam; maiden.

Peter Follenaer, from Hasselt.

Cornelis Michielsen, from Medemblick.

Grietje Christians, from Tonningen.

Claes Jansen, from Purmerend ; wheelwright, and wife, servant and child.

Marten van de Wert, from Utrecht ; hatter.

Peter van Ecke; planter, from Leyden.

Jacobus vander Schelling, and his boy.

Albert Theunissen vermeulen, from Rotterdam, and wife and four children.

Geertry van Meulen : maiden.

Hannetje Ruytenbeck, maiden.

Matthew Andriessen, from Peters-houck.

Hendrick Theunisz Hellinck and wife.

Lawrens van der Spiegel van Vlissingen.

DITTO ; *In the Moesman.*

Lysbeth Arents, wife of Corn : Barents, and daughter.

Aertje Leenders ; widow, from Amsterdam.

Barent van Loo from Elburg.

Willem Jansen, from Rotterdam, Fisherman, and wife and sucking child, and maid servant.

Peter Petersen, alias Pia, from Picardy, and wife and daughter.

Dirch Belet, from Breda; cooper.

Louis Aertz, from Bruges; planter.

Gerrit Corn. van Niew-Kierk, and wife and boy and sucking child.

Engelbrecht Sternhuysen, from Soest; tailor.

Thys Jansen, from TerGouw; agriculturist.

Albert Petersen, mason.

Geerty Claesen.

Gerrit Petersen.

Gillis Mandeville.

DECEMBER; *In the Faith.*

Christiaen de Lorie, from St. Malo.

Hendrick Jansen Spiers and wife and two children.

Adriaen Huybertsen Sterrevelt; agriculturist.

Harmen Stepfer, from the Dutchy of Cleef.

Joost Adriaensen Pynacker, from Delft.

Philip Langelens; agriculturist, and wife and two children.

Hendrick Bos, from Leyden, and wife and two children.

Gerrit Gerritsen, from Wageningen, and wife and one child.

William Aertsen, from Wagening.

Gerrit van Manen, from Wagening.

Albert Gerritsen, from Wagening.

Jan Gerritsen Hagel.

Hendrick Jansen, from Wagening.

Jan Aertsen, from Amersfoort.

Jacob Jansen, from Amersfoort.

Tys Jansen, from Amersfoort.

Wessel Wesselsen, from Munster.

Adolph Hardenbroeck, and wife and son.

Claes Theunissen, from Gorcum, and his servant, and boy.

Lubbert Harmensen, from Overyssel.

Lammert Huybertsen, from Wagening, and wife and two children.

Jan Harmans and wife and sucking child.

Roeloft Hendricks from Drenthe.

Femmetje Hendricksen, maiden.

Maria Mooris, from Arnhem, maiden.

Marten Abrahamsen, from Bloemendael, and wife and two children.

The wife of Hans Sodurat, baker, and two children.

Leendert Arentsen Groenevelt, and wife.

Aeltje Jacobsen; maiden.

Willem Petersen, from Amersfoort.

Claes Tysen; cooper, and two children.

B

1660.

MARCH ; *In the Love.*

Wiggert Reinders, from Ter Gouw; farmer.
Maritje Jansen maiden.
Bart Jansen, from Amsterdam; mason, and wife
and three children.
Cornelis Davitsen Schaets; wheel right.
Laurens Harmens, from Holstein and wife.
Dirck Gerritsen vandien from Tricht; agriculturer.

DITTO; *In the Moesman.*

Peter Lourens and wife.
Hendrick Jansen, from Amersfoort, and wife and
four children.

DITTO ; *In the Gilded Beaver.*

Annetje Abrahams ; maiden.
Cornelis Niesen's wife.
Jonas Bartesen, and wife and two children.
Maria Jans; orphan daughter.

APRIL; *In the Spotted Cow.*

Jan Soubanich, from Byle in Drenthe.

Albert Janss; from Drenthe.

Peter Jacobs, from East Friesland.

Cornelis Bartels, from Drenthe.

Steven Koorts, from Drenthe and wife and seven children.

Jan Kevers, from the Landscape Drenthe, and wife.

Focke Jansen from Drenthe; agriculturist, and wife and seven children.

Claes Arentsen, from Drenthe, and wife and three children, and boy.

Govert Egberts, from Meppelt, farmer's servant.

Evertje Dircks, from Drenthe; maiden.

Egbertje Dircks, from Drenthe; maiden.

Peter Jansen; shoemaker from Drenthe, and wife and four children.

Coert Cartens, from Drenthe, farmer's servant.

Roeloft Swartwout; agriculturist. [On his return to N. Netherland where he had previously resided.]

Cornelis Jacobs van Leeuwen; in the service of Swartwout.

Arent Meuwens, from Gelderland; in Swartwout's service.

Ariaen Huyberts, from Jena; in Swartwout's service.

Peter Hinham, from Nimwegen; tailor.

Albert Heymans; agriculturist, from Gelderland
and wife and eight children.
Jan Jacobsen Mol.
Annetje Harmens; maiden.
Beletje Foppe.
Elias Gyseling, from Zealand.

*Roll of Soldiers embarked in the Ship
Moesman, for New Netherland,
9th March, 1660.*

Peter Gysen from Doornick Adelborst, with his
wife.
Harmen Hendricks from Deventer.
William vander Beecke from Oudenaerde.
Jacob Jansen from Muyden.
Andries Norman from Steenwyck.
Marten Petersen from Steenwyck.
Jan God-frien l from Brussel.
Jan Jansen from Duynkerken.
Pieter Beyard from Nieupoort.
Willem van Schure from Leuven.
Adrianus Forbiet from Brussel.
Johannis Verele from Antwerp.
Matthys Princen from Waltneel.

List of Soldiers embarked in the Ship the Spotted Cow, 15th April, 1660.

Claes Petersen, Adelborst from Detmarsum.
Claes Hayen from Bremen.

Soldiers.

Jan Petersen from Detmarsen.
Gerrit Manneel van Haen.
Conract Croos from Switserland.
Hendrick Eyck from Srahuys.
Christian Bartels Ruysh from Amsterdam.
Hendrich Steveterinck from Osnasnigge.
Peter Martens from Laens.
John Hamelton of Hamelton.
Johan Verpronck from Bonn above Ceulen; a
smith and baker.
Jan Wilekheresen from Bergen in Norway.
Peter Petersen from Amsterdam, with his wife and
two children.
Brant Kemenes from Dockum.
Dirck jansen from Rylevelt.
Harman Jansen Engsinck from Oldenseel.
Johannes Levelin from Bulhausen.
Michiel Brouwnal from (Berg) Mont-eassel.

List of Soldiers, embarked for New Netherland in the Ship Otter, 27th April 1660.

Jan Vresen, from Hamburg; Adelborst, and wife and two children.

Jacob Loyseler, from Francfort.

Daniel Lengelgraast, from Amsterdam.

Thomas Vorstuyt, from Bremen.

Harmen Hellings, from Verda.

Gysbert Dircksen, from Schans te voorn.

Teunis Warten, from Gorcum.

Ferdinandus Willays, from Cortryck.

Reinier Cornelis, from Utrect, to be discharged whenever he request it, to follow his trade.

Joost Kockeiot, from Wrimigen.

Jan Vaex, from Nieustad.

Jan Vier, from Bon.

Jan Claesen, from Outserenter.

Paulus Mettermans, from L'Orient.

Peter Teunis, from Steenburg.

IMMIGRANTS; *In the Gilded Otter.*

Joost Huyberts, from Gelderland; agriculturist, and wife and two children.

Philip Cassier, from Calais; agriculturist, and wife and four children.

David Uplie, from Calais; agriculturist, and wife.

Matthews Blanchard, from Artois; agriculturist, and wife and three children.

Jan Adriaensen van Duyvelant's wife.

Anthony Krypel, from Artois; agriculturist, and wife.

Canster Jacob's wife, from Hoesem and daughter.

Willem Jacobsen, from Haerlem; agriculturist.

Bastiaen Glissen, from Calemburg; agriculturist and wife and five children.

Gerrit Janz van Veen, from Calemburg; farmer's boy.

Gerrit Aartsen van Buren; agriculturist.

Gerrit Cornelissen van Buren; agriculturist.

Cornelis Abrahams, from Gelderland; agriculturist.

1661.

JANUARY; *In the Golden Eagle.*

Cornelis Gerlossen, from East Friesland; tailor.
Jannetje Barents, widow of Jan Quisthout.
Jacob Farments, wife and child.

MAY; *In the Beaver.*

Hugh Barentsen de Clein, and wife and seven children.

Peter Marcelis van Beest, and wife and four children and two servants.

Aert Pietersen Buys van Beest, and wife and son.

Franz Jacobsen van Beest, and wife and two children.

Widow Geertje Cornelis van Beest, and six children.

Widow Adriaentje Cornelis van Beest, and daughter.

Goossen Jansen van Noort van Beest.

Hendrick Dries van Beest.

Neeltje Jans van Beest.

Geertruy Teunissen van Beest.

Geertje Willems, from Amsterdam.
Aert Teunnissen Middagh.
Jacob Bastiaensen, from Heycop.
Estienne Genejoy, from Rochelle, and wife and three children.
Jan Lammertsen, from Bremen.
Hendrickje Jochems.
Geertje Jochems.
Wouter Thysen, from Hilversom.
Gideon Jacobs.
The Son of Evertson, Consoler of the sick.

DITTO; *In the St. Jean Baptist.*

Gerrit Gerritsen, from Besevenn.
Gommert Paulessen from Antwerp.
Aerent Teunissen, from Amsterdam, and wife and two children.
Jan Theunissen, from Amsterdam, and wife and two children.
Annetje van Genen, from Sinden.
Geertje Samsons, from Weesp.
Jan Willemson, from the Loosdrecht, and wife and two sons.
Peter Bielliou, from Pays de vaud, and wife and four children.

Walraven Luten, from Flanders, and wife and suckling.

Mynder Coerten from Adighem.

Claes Jansen, from Uithoorn and wife and child.

Andries Imans, from Leyden.

Jacob Abrahamsen Santvoort.

Gerrit Hendricksen, from Swoll.

Tys Barentsen, from Leirdam, and wife and three children.

Cornelis Dircksen Vos from Leirdam, and wife, mother and two children.

NOVEMBER; *In the Purmerland Church.*

Barent Cornellissen Slecht.

1662.

JANUARY; *In the Golden Eagle.*

Peter Jansen Cuyck, from Heusden, agriculturist.
Peter Jansen, from Amsterdam ; agriculturist.
Teunis Dircksen Boer, and wife and three children.
Seiwart Petersen, from Hoesem ; malster.

MARCH; *In the Faith.*

Lysbet Harmens, from the Traert.
Jan Gerrits, from Embden ; labourer.
Jacob Wouters, from Amsterdam.
Barent Witten Hooft, from Munster, tailor, and
wife and two children.
Stoffel Smet, from Keurlo ; agriculturist.
Adriaen Hendricks, from Borckelo ; agriculturist.
Precilla Homes, and her brother, and one suckling.
Thomas Harmensen Brouwers, from Sevenburgen ;
farmer.
Symon Cornie ; farmer from France, and wife.
Adriaen Gerritsen, from Utrecht ; agriculturist,
and wife and five children.

Albert Jansen, from Steenwyck ; tailor.

Reinier Petersen, from Steenwyck ; agriculturer.

Claes van Campen, from Oldenburg ; farmer's boy.

Adriaen Aartsen from Thillerwarden in Guilderland.

Hendrick Arentsen, from the same place; labourer.

April ; *In the Hope.*

Annetje Hendricks, wife of Jan Evertsen ; shoemaker, and five children.

Cornelis Dircksen Hooglant ; agriculturer, and wife, son and daughter.

Jacob Jansen ; N. Netherland ; farmer, and wife and three children.

Adriaen Vincian, from Toornay; agriculturer.

Jochem Engelburgh, from Heusden.

Gerrit Hargerinck, from Newenhuys, and two sons.

Annetje Gillis van Beest; servant girl.

Jan Petersen, from Deventer ; tailor, and wife and three children.

Jan Timmer, from Gorekum, and wife.

Luytje Gerrits ; agriculturist from Friesland.

Peckle Dircksen, from Friesland.

Willem Lubbertsen, from Meppel ; agriculturist, and wife and six children.

Lubbert Lubbertsen, from Meppel; agriculturist, and wife and four children.

Jan Barentsen, from Meppel; agriculturist, and wife and five children.

Gerrit Jacobsen, from Meppel; agriculturist.

Harmtje Barents, from Meppel; maiden.

Willem Pietersen de Groot, and wife and five children.

Abel Hardenbroeck, and wife and child, and servant named Casper Overcamp.

Balthaser de Vos, from Utrecht; farmer, and wife.

Hendrick Aldertsen, from the Thillerwaerd; farmer, and two children.

Albert Buer, from Gulick.

Jan Spiegelaer, and wife.

AUGUST; *In the Fox.*

Jan de la Warde, from Antwerp.

Albert Saboriski, from Prussia.

Anthony Dircksen, from Brabant.

Pierre Martin, Pays de Vaud.

Gerardus Ive, from Pays de Vaud.

Joost Grand, from Pays de Vaud.

Jan Le chaire, from Valenciennes; carpenter.

Jan Albantsen, from Steenwyck, and wife and child.

Ammereus Claesen, maiden.

Hendrick Albertsen; labourer.

Jan Claesen; labourer.

Lysbet Hendricksen.

Jan Bossch, from Westphalen.

Roelof Hermansen, from Germany, and wife.

Robbert de la Main, from Dieppe.

David Kraffort; mason, and wife and child.

Jacomyntje Jacobs, daughter of Jacob Swart.

Juriaen Jansen, from Holstein.

Annetje Anthonis, wife of Gerrit Mannaet, and her child.

Souverain Ten Houte; baker.

Albert Hendricksen, from Maersen; house carpenter.

Symon Scholts, from Prussia.

Hendrick Tymensen, from Loodrecht.

David Ackerman, from the Mayory of Bosch, and wife and six children.

Willem Symonsen, from Amsterdam.

Pierre de Marc, from Rouen; shoemaker.

Dirck Storm, from the Mayory of Bosch, and wife and three children.

David Davidsen, from Maestricht.

Jan Jootsen, from the Thielerwaert, and wife and five children.

Claes Barents, from Dort.

Lendert Dircksen Van Venloo, of Rumunt.

Adreaen Lowrensen Van Loesren, carpenter.

OCTOBER; *In the Purmerland Church.*

Claus Paulus, from Detmarsum, and wife.

Nicolas du Pui, from Artois, and wife and three children.

Arnout du Tois, from Ryssel, (Lisle,) and wife and one child.

Gideon Merlit, and wife and four children.

Louis Louhman, and wife and three children.

Jacques Cossaris, and wife and two children.

Jan de Conchilier, (now, Consilyea) and wife and five children.

Jacob Colff, from Leyden, and wife and two children.

Judith Jans, from Leyden, maiden.

Carsten Jansen.

Ferdinandus de Mulder.

Isaac Verniel, and wife and four children.

Abelis Setshoorn.

Claes Jansen van Heynengen.

1663.

MARCH; *In the Rosetree.*

Andries Pietersen van Bergen.

Dirck Everts, from Amersfoort, and wife and three children.

Peter Jansen, from Amersfoort, and four children.

Frederick Claesen, from Norway.

Jeremias Jansen, from Westerhoot.

Jan Jacobsen, from East Friesland, and wife and two children.

Hendrick Hendricksen, from Westphalia.

Hendrick Lammerts, from Amersfoort.

Jan Jansen Verberck, from Buren, and wife and five children.

Jannetje Willemsen.

Adrian Lammertsen, from Tielderveen, and wife and six children.

Jacob Hendricks, his nephew.

Theunis Jansen, from the country of Liege, and wife and six children.

Thys Jansen, from the country of Liege, and four children.

Theunis Gerritsen; painter, from Buren.

Jan Petersen Buys van Beest.

Hendrick Hansen, from Germany.

Edward Smith, from Leyden.

Peter Martensen, from Ditmarsum, and child.

Bay Groesvelt, and wife and sucking child.

Cornelis Claesen, from Amsterdam.

Hendrick Abels, from Leyden.

Barent Holst, from Hamburgh.

Hendrick Wessels, from Wishem.

C aes Wouters, from Amersfoort, and wife and one child.

Grietje Hendricks, wife of Jan Arentsen Smith in Esopus and daughter.

Jan Cornelisz van Limmigen.

Hendrick Jansen; painter.

Grietje Harmens, from Alckmaer.

Fredrick Claesen, from Mespelen.

Ditto; *In the Eagle.*

Willem Schot.

Elias Jansen, from Tiel.

Dirck Schiltman, from Tiel.

Andrees Petersen, from Tiel.

Maria Laurens.

Grietje Jaspers, from Tiel ; maiden.

Dirck Lucas.

Clement Rosens.

Evert Dirksen, from Vianen, and two children.

APRIL ; *In the Spotted Cow.*

Hendrick Corneliss, from New Netherland.

Staes de Groot, from Tricht.

Elje Barents, the wife of Adam Bremen, and servant girl.

Jan Lourens, from Schoonder Woort, and wife and two children.

Theunis Bastiaensen Cool, and child.

Jan Bastiaensen, from Leerdam, and wife and four children.

Giel Bastiaensen, from Leerdam, and wife and four children.

Gerrit Jans, from Arnhem, and wife and brother-in-law, Arnoldus Willems.

Joris Adriaensen, from Leerdam.

Peter Matthysen, from Limborg h.

Jan Boerhans.

Lammert Jansen Dorlant.

Gerrit Verbeeck.

Grietje Gerrits, the wife of Dirck Jansen, and two children.

Adriaen Jansen Honink, from Well, and wife and four children.

Hans Jacob Sardingh.

Juriaen Tomassen, from Rypen.

Jan Laurens, from Rypen.

Jan Otto van Teyl, and wife and child.

Matthys Bastiaensen vander Peich, and daughter.

Marytje Theunis van Beest.

Jerome Bovie, from Pays de Vaud, and wife and five children.

David de Marist, from Picardy, and wife and four children.

Pierre Niu, from the Pays de Vaud, and wife, sucking child and sister.

Jean Mesurole, from Picardy, and wife and sucking child.

Jean Arien, from Montpellier, and wife and child (removed to the islands).

Martin Renare, from Picardy, and wife and child.

Jacob Kerve, from Leyden, and wife.

Pierre Parmentie, from Pays de Vaud, and wife and son.

Joost Houpleine, from Flanders, and wife and son.

Joost Houpleine, junior, and wife and sucking child.

Guilliam Goffou, from Sweden.

Moillart Journay, from Pays de Vaud.

Pierre Richard, from Paris.

JUNE; *In the Star*.

Peter Worster.
Vieu Pont, from Normandy.
Joan Paul de Rues.

DITTO; *In the St. Jacob*.

Geertje Huyberts, wife of Jan Gerritsen, from Marken, and nephew.
Annetje Jacobs, from Gornichem.

SEPTEMBER; *In the Stetin*.

Schout Olferts, from Friesland, and wife and child and servant Foppe Johannis.
Jacob Govertsen, and son.
Jan Jansen, the younger, and wife and child.
Claes Jansen, from Amsterdam, and wife and three children.
Anthoni Berghman, from Gorcum.
Hendrick Gerretsen, from Aernhem.

Willem Van Voorst, from Arnhem.

Grietje Jansen, from Weldorp.

Cornelis Teunissen, from Norway.

Peter Carstensen, from Holsteyn, and son.

Jacob Bastiaensen, from Newerveen.

Jan Jansen, from Norway, and wife.

Grietje Hargeringh, Jan Hargeringh, from Newenhuys.

Johannes Burger, from Geemen.

Gysbert Krynne Boelhont.

Beletje Jacobs, van Naerden.

Reinier Claesen, from Francken.

Hessel Megelis, from Friesland.

Jan Laurense, from New Netherland.

Albert Adriaense de Bruyn, from the Betawe.

Dirck Teunissen van Naerden.

Jan Vreesen, from Hamburg.

Jan Roelofsen, from Norway.

Susanna Verplanck, and child.

Lysbet ver Schuren.

Jan Brouwer, and brother.

Annetje Hendricks, wife of Fredrick Hendricks Cooper.

Douwe Aukes.

Merine Johannis, and wife and four children together with his wife's sister and his servant.   ,

October; *In the St. Peter.*

Marritje Jans, from Amsterdam.

Boel Roelofs, from Friesland.

Peter Alberts, from Vlissingen, and wife and two children.

Ariaen Peters Kume, from Fiissingen.

Willem Luycass, from Maeslands-sluys.

1664.

JANUARY; *In the Faith.*

Marcelis Jansen van Bommel; farmer.

Evert Tack, from the Barony of Breda.

Lysbet Arens, from Amsterdam, and child.

Johannis Hardenbroeck, from Elberveld, and wife and four children.

Janneken Juriaensen, from Gorcum.

Corneliss Cornelissen Vernoey, and wife and sucking child.

Lysbet de Roode, from Dantzick, wife of John Saline, and child.

Sara Teunis.

DITTO; *In the Broken Heart.*

Lysbeth Jansen van Wie, near Goch.

The wife of Govert van Oy, and two children.

Jan Jansen, from Amsterdam.

Claes Gerritsen, son of Gerrit Lubbertsen, from Wesel.

S. Vander Wessels.

Jan Wouterse van Norden.

DITTO ; *In the Beaver.*

Anietje Hendricks van der Briel.

APRIL ; *In the Concord.*

Abigel Verplanck, and child.

Claes Mellis, from Great Schermer, and wife and two children and servant.

Jan Taelman.

Hendrick Bartholomeus and five children.

Claes Gerritsen, and wife and child.

Jentje Jeppes, and wife and three children.

Bastiaen Corneliss, from Maersen.

Maes Willems, from Heyland.

The wife of Jan Evertsen van Lier, and child.

Claes Andriessen, from Holsteyn.

Gerrit Gerritsen, from Swol.

Sicke Jans, from Amsterdam.

Seravia vander Hagen, and child.

Carel Enjoert, from Flanders, and wife and three children.

Hendrick Wienrick, from Wesel.

Adriaentje Hendricks, and child.

END OF VOL I.

First Settlement of the New Netherlands.

[COLLECTANEA ADAMANTÆA. XXVII.]

PAPERS RELATING TO

THE

First Settlement of New York

BY THE DUTCH,

CONTAINING

*A LIST OF THE EARLY IMMIGRANTS
TO NEW NETHERLAND;*

1657-1664.

From the " Documentary History of New York,"

AND

The Description and First Settlement of New Netherland,

From " Wassenaer's Historie van Europa."

IN TWO VOLUMES.
VOL. II.

PRIVATELY PRINTED.
EDINBURGH.
1888.

Wassenaer's description of
New Netherland.

FIRST SETTLEMENT OF NEW NETHERLAND.

[From Wassenaer's Historie van Europa.]

NUMEROUS voyages realize so much profit for adventurers that they discover other countries, which they afterwards settle and plant. Virginia, a country lying in 42½ degrees, is one of these. It was first peopled by the French; afterwards by the English, and is to-day a flourishing colony. The Lords States General observing the great abundance of their people as well as their desire to plant other lands, allowed the West India company to settle that same country. Many from the United Colonies did formerly and do still trade there;—yea, for the greater security of the traders, a castle—Fort Nassau—had been built on an island in 42 degrees, on the north side of the river Montagne, now called Mauritius. But as the natives there were somewhat discontented, and not easily managed, the projectors abandoned it, intending now to plant a colony among the Maikans a nation lying 25 miles* on both sides of the river, upwards.

This river, or the bay, lies in 40 degrees, running well in ; being as broad or wide as the Thames, and navigable fully fifty miles up, through divers nations, who sometimes manifest themselves with arrows, like enemies, sometimes like friends ; but when they had seen the ships once or twice, or traded with our people, they became altogether friendly.

Below the Maikans are situate these tribes ; Mechkentowoon, Tapants, on the west side ; Wiekagjock, Wyeck on the east side. Two nations lie there lower down at Klinckersberg. At the Fisher's hook are Pachany, Warenecker Warra. wannankonckx : In one place, Esopes, are two or three tribes. The Manhates are situate at the mouth. In the interior are also many, as the Maquas. Full fifty miles further are found likewise many villages, all which come to this river to trade from the interior which is very swampy, great

---

*The miles stated in this paper are Dutch.

quantities of water running to the river, over-flowing the adjoining country, which was frequently the cause that Fort Nassau lay under water and was abandoned.

This country now called NEW NETHERLAND is usually reached in seven or eight weeks from here. The course lies towards the Canary Islands; thence to the Indian Islands, then towards the main land of Virginia, steering right across, leaving in fourteen days the Bahamas on the left, and the Bermudas on the right hand where the winds are variable with which the land is made.

Respecting religion we as yet cannot learn that they have any knowledge of God, but there is something similar in repute among them. What they have is set over them by the "Cabal" from ancestor to ancestor. They say that mention was made by their forefathers for many thousand moons, of good and evil spirits, to whose honour, it is supposed, they burn fires or sacrifices. They wish to stand well with the good spirits; they like exhortations about them. The Ministry of their spiritual affairs is attended to by one they call Kitzinacka, which, I think, is priest. When any one among them is sick, he visits him; sits by him and bawls, roars and cries like one possessed. If a man die, he is laid in the earth without a coffin, with all his costly garments of skins. This priest has no house of his own. He lodges where

he pleases, or where he last officiated ; must not
eat any food prepared by a married woman. It
must be cooked by a maiden or old woman. He
never cohabits with them, living like a capuchin.
When a child arrives at the age of twelve, then
they can determine whether he shall be a Kitsi·
nacka or not. If tis so ruled, then he is elevated
to such office. Becoming of age, he undertakes
the exercise of it.

All the natives pay particular attention to the
sun, the moon, and the stars, as they are of as
great interest to them, as to us, having like
summer and winter. But geographers are aware
that the length and shortness of the days differ, on
account of situation. The first moon following
that at the end of February is greatly honored by
them. They watch it with great devotion, and
as it rises they compliment it with a festival ; then
they collect together from all quarters, and revel
in their way, with wild game or fish, and drink
clear river water to their fill, without being intoxi-
cated. It appears that the year commences then,
this moon being a harbinger of the spring. Shortly
afterwards the women begin to prepare what is to
be for food by planting, putting everything in a
state of preparation, and carrying their seed into
the field. They allow the succeeding moons to
appear without any feasting ; but they celebrate
the new August moon by another festival, as their

harvest then approaches. It is very abundant in
consequence of the great mildness of the climate.
The summers are frequently very hot, and the
land moist, which produces abundance of fruit
and grain. Indian corn is abundant there, and
is pounded by the women, made into meal, and
baked into cakes in the ashes, after the olden
fashion, and used for food.

As they care nothing for the spiritual, they
direct their study principally to the physical,
closely observing the seasons. The women there
are the most experienced star gazers; there is
scarcely one of them but can name all the stars;
their rising, setting; the position of the Arctos,
that is the wagon, is as well known to them as to
us, and they name them by other names. But
Him who dwells above they know not; affording
all us Christians an argument to thank Him, that
He hath so beneficently favored us, leaving these
in darkness; so that what the apostle says is found
to be true. It is not of him that willeth, nor of
him that runneth, but of God that sheweth mercy.*

There is little authority known among these
nations. They live almost all free. In each
village, indeed, is found a person who is somewhat above the others and commands absolutely
when there is war and when they are gathered

---

* Rom. ix.

from all the villages to go on the war path.   But
the fight once ended, his superiority ceases.   They
are very much afraid of the dead ; but when they
perceive that they must die, they are very brave
and more ferocious than beasts.   When a lad
courts a girl, he buys her generally in a neighbor-
ing village, and this done, the daughter is then
delivered to him by two or three other women,
who come carrying on their heads meal, roots,
corn and other articles, to the young man's hut,
and he receives her.   The dwellings are commonly
circular ; with a vent hole above to let out the
smoke ; closed with four doors, consisting most of
the bark of trees which are very abundant there.
They sleep on the ground covered with leaves and
skins.   At their meals they sit on the ground.
Each highly esteems his own children, who grow
up very lively.   The women sew skins into clothing, prepare bread, cook the meat which the men
hunt and kill with arrows, especially in the winter
when all is bare in the fields and but scanty forage
is to be picked off the snow ; then the animals
approach the villages and are shot.

It is very common among them for one man to
buy and to have many wives, but not in one
place ; when he journeys five or six miles he finds
another wife who also takes care of him ; five or
ten miles further, he again finds another wife who
keeps house and so on to several ; commonly

buying up peltries through the country. But as those inland find that furs are sold cheap among them, they come down themselves to the rivers and trade with the nations as best they can. Also those who will trade with them must furnish them food at an inhabitant's in the village—let them cook their meat and fish there, as much as they like, and then they thank the trader. In other respects, they are extremely hospitable; the one lodges with the other without any ceremony, on similar compensation. Those who come from the interior, yea thirty days journey, declare there is considerable water every where and that the upper country.is marshy; they make mention of great freshets which lay waste their lands; so that what many say may be true, that Hudson's Bay runs through to the South Sea, and is navigable, except when obstructed by the ice to the northward. It were desirable that it were once proved. Those who made the last voyage are of the same opinion, as they found all open sea, a rapid current and whales.

They live in summer mostly on fish. The men repair to the river and catch a great quantity in a short time, as it is full and furnishes various sorts. The arrows they use are pointed with little bones, iron or copper, with which they are very expert, being good marksmen. They can catch deer, fawns, hares and foxes and all such. The country is full of game; hogs, bears, leopards, yea lions, as appears by the skins which were brought on board. Oxen and horses there are none.

In the woods are found all sorts of fruits; plums, wild cherries, pears; yea, fruits in great profusion. Tobacco is planted in abundance, but much better grows wild in Brazil; it is called Virginian. Vines grow wild there; were there vintagers and were they acquainted with the press, good wine could be brought hither in great quantity, and even as Must, the voyage thence being often made in thirty days.

Their trade consists mostly in peltries, which they measure by the hand or by the finger. It happened that a woman who had seen a skipper's lace shirt, fell sick; finding she should die, she gave her husband three fine peltry skins to present to the skipper for the shirt, which he willingly gave her, for she wished to be buried in it; they outstrip the Christians in the sumptuousness of their burials. In exchange for peltries they receive beads, with which they decorate their persons; knives, adzes, axes, case-knives, kettles and all sorts of iron work which they require for house keeping.

In their waters are all sorts of fowls, such as cranes, bitterns, swans, geese, ducks, widgeons, wild geese, as in this country. Birds fill also the

woods so that men can scarcely go through them
for the whistling, the noise, and the chattering.
Whoever is not lazy can catch them with little
difficulty. Turkey beans is a very common crop.
Pigeons fly wild, they are chased by the foxes
like fowls. Tortoises are very small, and are not
eaten, because there is plenty of other food. The
most wonderful are the bull-frogs, in size about a
span, which croak with a ringing noise in the
evening, as in this country. 'Tis surprising that
storks have not been found there, if it be a marshy
country. Spoonbills, ravens, eagles, sparrow-
hawks, vultures are numerous and are actually
shot or knocked down by the natives.

'Tis worthy of remark that so great a diversity
of language exists among the numerous tribes.
They vary frequently not over five or six miles;
forthwith comes another language; they meet and
can hardly understand one another. There are
some who come sixty miles from the interior, and
can not well understand those on the river. All
are very cunning in trade; yea, frequently, after
having sold every thing, they will go back of the
bargain, and that forcibly, in order to get a little
more; and then they return upwards, being thirty
and forty strong; their outer clothing being all
skins and furs.

It appears by the statements of the Highlanders,
there are larger animals in the interior. On seeing

the head of *Taurus*, one of the signs of the zodiac, the women know how to explain that it is a horned head of a big, wild animal which inhabits the distant country, but not their's, and when it rises in a certain part of the heavens, at a time known to them, then is the season for planting ; then they begin to break up the soil with axes *(bylen)* and to throw in the seed ; like the Boors in Italy who appear by Virgil *in Bucolicis* to take their proper time from the signs.

The science of prognostication, or foretelling of events is altogether dark and unknown to them ; uttering or delivering no oracles about the one or the other, as they have very little knowledge of future or past things.

What's very strange is, that among these almost barbarous people, there are few or none, cross-eyed, blind, crippled, lame, hunch-backed or limping ; all are well fashioned people ; strong in constitution of body, well proportioned without blemish.

In some places they have abundant means, with herbs and leaves or roots, to administer to their sick.   There is scarcely an ailment they have not a remedy for ; but in other localities they are altogether devoid of succour, leaving the people to perish like cattle.

Chastity appears to be of some repute among them, for the women are not all equally loose

There are some who would not cohabit with ours for any compensation. Others hold it in small esteem ; especially as they are free, living without law. Whilst rearing their offspring, they exhibit great tenderness ; nevertheless as children rapidly increase with these people, they forbid theirs (the house) as not beseeming; yea, command them not to return back.

They are not, by nature, the most gentle. Were there no weapons, especially muskets, near, they would frequently kill the traders for the sake of the plunder ; but whole troops run before five or six muskets. At the first coming (of the whites) they were accustomed to fall prostrate on the report of the gun ; but now they stand still from habit, so that the first colonists will stand in need of protection.

The South-bay,* some miles nearer Florida, is a more temperate country. There is no winter there save in January, and then but for a few days.

Their numerals run no higher than ours ; twenty being twice ten. When they ask for twenty, they stick the ten fingers up and with them turn to the feet on which are ten toes. They count, Honslat, Tegeni, Hasse, Kajeri, Wisk, Jajack, Satach, Siattege, Tiochte, Ojeri.†

---

* Delaware Bay.
† The author of this paper must have obtained his

The names of their months are these;—Cuerano, the first with them, February: 2. Weer-hemska : 3. Heemskan: 4. Oneratacka : 5. Oneratack, then men begin to sow and to plant : 6. Hagarert: 7. Iacouvaratta: 8. Hatterhonagat: 9. Genhendasta : then the grain and everything is ripe. 10. Digojenjattha, then is the seed housed. Of January and December they take no note, being of no use to them.

A ship was fitted out under a commission from the West India Company, and freighted with families, to plant a colony among this people. But to go in safety, it is first of all necessary that they be placed in a good defensive position and well provided with arms and a fort, as the Spaniard who claims all the country, will never allow any one to gain a possession there ; and as the Spaniards have made many incursions as well above as below, in Florida, Virginia, and thereabouts, I deem it not foreign to tell something thereof, being a mirror in which every one can see and defend himself, and how the Spaniards always aim as well generally as individually at Monarchy. Such description shall be related in the com-

---

information from some Iroquois, as with the exception of the first, these are the names of the numerals according to the Mohawk and Onondaga dialects. The last (Ojeri) approaches the Seneca.

mencement of Part the Seventh, as this Book
cannot contain it.

~~~~~~~~~~~~~~~~~~

Homo est animal sociable, is in some sense a
definition; in some sense a description, of man.
Men's sociability led them to congregate and to
live peaceably together, from which arose hamlets,
villages and cities, and afterwards chiefs were
chosen among them. These remarking that the
collected heaps frequently so increased that they
could with difficulty support themselves, a portion
separated therefrom, who took up and settled the
neighbouring places. The patriarchs of the Old
Testament, finding themselves altogether too many
in their country, sent some of theirs into the
uninhabited valleys, and cultivated these accordingly. The Assyrians wishing to enlarge their
monarchy caused their subjects to inhabit the
invaded countries in great numbers. Those of
the Persian monarchy did no less. But the
Greeks extended their limits very far; for they
by navigation peopled entire islands, as appears

by the highly learned Petrus Cluverius, who furnishes us correct information on all points in his published Italy.* The Romans domineering over the western world, spread colonies all over it, as is proved by the excavated stones found every where; but what order they observed herein is well known to us. Those sent thither, must acknowledge the senders as their lords, pay them homage, and remain under their sovereignty; they were also protected by these by suitable weapons furnished also to them. And whereas, God be praised, it hath so prospered that the Honorable Lords Directors of the West India Company have, with the consent of the Noble High and Mighty Lords States General, under-taken to plant some colonies, I shall give the particulars of them, as follows :—

We treated in our preceding discourse of the discovery of some rivers in Virginia ; the studious reader will learn how affairs proceeded. The West India Company being chartered to navigate these rivers, did not neglect so to do, but equipped in the spring [of 1623] a vessel of 130 lasts, called the *New Netherland* whereof Cornelis Jacobs of Hoorn was skipper, with 30 families, mostly Walloons, to plant a colony there. They sailed

---

* Italia Antiqua. Ex officina E seviriana 1624. Folio.

in the beginning of March, and directing their
course by the Canary Islands, steered towards the
wild coast, and gained the westwind which luckily
(took) them in the beginning of May into the
river called, first Rio de Montagnes, now the
river Mauritius, lying in 40½ degrees. He found
a Frenchman lying in the mouth of the river, who
would erect the arms of the King of France there;
but the Hollanders would not permit him, oppos-
ing it by commission from the Lords States
General and the directors of the West India
Company; and in order not to be frustrated
therein, with the assistance of those of the
Mackerel which lay above, they caused a yacht
of 2 guns to be manned, and convoyed the
Frenchman out of the river, who would do the
same thing in the south river, but he was also
prevented by the settlers there.

This being done, the ship sailed up to the
Maykans, 44 miles, near which they built and
completed a fort named "Orange" with 4 bastions,
on an island, by them called Castle Island. They
forthwith put the spade in the ground and began
to plant, and before the Mackerel sailed, the grain
was nearly as high as a man, so that they are
bravely advanced. They placed also a fort named
"Wilhelmus" on Prince's Island, heretofore called
Murderer's Island; it is open in front, and has a
curtain in the rear and is garrisoned by sixteen

men for the defence of the river below. On
leaving there, the course lies for the west wind,
and having got it, to the Bermudas and so along
the channel in a short time towards Patria. The
yacht, the Mackerel, sailed out last year on the
16th June and arrived yonder on the 12th of
December. That was somewhat late, but it
wasted time in the Indian Islands, to catch fish,
and did not catch any, so lost this opportunity.
The Honble. Daniel Van Krieckebeeck, for brevity
called, Beeck, was Commissary here, and so did
his duty that he was thanked.

Respecting these colonies, they have already a
prosperous beginning ; and the hope is that they
will not fall through provided they be zealously
sustained, not only in that place but in the South
river.   For their increase and prosperous advance-
ment, it is highly necessary that those sent out be
first of all well provided with means both of
support and defence, and that being freemen,
they be settled there on a free tenure; that all
they work for and gain be their's to dispose of
and to sell it according to their pleasure; that
whoever is placed over them as commander act as
their father not as their executioner, leading them
with a gentle hand ; for whoever rules them as a
friend and associate will be beloved by them, as
he who will order them as a superior will subvert
and nullify every thing; yea, they will excite

against him the neighbouring provinces to which they will fly. 'Tis better to rule by love and friendship than by force.

At the same time that the fleet arrived from Archangel, a large quantity of otter skins were received here in Amsterdam from France, finer than had ever been seen in this country. They were the product of Canada and the circumjacent places. The tribes are in the habit of clothing themselves with them ; the fur or hair inside, the smooth side without, which, however, they paint so beautifully that, at a distance, it resembles lace. It is the opinion that they make use of the best for that purpose ; what has poor fur they deem unsuitable for their clothing. When they bring their commodities to the traders, and find they are desirous to buy them, they make so very little matter of it, that they at once rip up the skins they are clothed with and sell them as being the best. They use beaver skins mostly for the sleeves, as they are not so expensive ; and they frequently come several days journey from the interior, to exchange theirs with the tribes.

Agriculture progresses in New Netherland in this wise. It is very pleasant, all products being in abundance, though wild. Grapes are of very good flavour, but will be, henceforward better cultivated by our people. Cherries are not found there. There are all sorts of fowls, both in the water and in the air. Swans, geese, ducks, bitterns, abound. The men scarcely ever labour, except to provide some game, either fowl or other description, for cooking, and then they have provided every thing. The women must attend to the remainder, tilling the soil, &c. When our people arrived there, they were busy cleaning up and planting. Before this vessel had left, the harvest was far advanced. It excites little attention if any one [of the Indians] abandon his wife; in case she have children, they usually follow her. Their summers are fine, but the days there are shorter than with us here. The winters are severe, but there is plenty of fuel, as the country is well wooded and it is at the service of whoever wants it.

Their is some respect paid to those in authority amongst them; but these are no wise richer than others. There is always so much ado about them that the chief is feared and obeyed as long as he is near, but he must shift for himself like others. There is nothing seen in his house more than in those of the rest.

As regards the prosperity of New Netherland, we learn by the arrival of the ship whereof Jan May of Hoorn, was skipper, that every thing there was in good condition. The colony began to advance bravely and continues in friendship with the natives. The fur, or other trade, remains in the West India company, others being forbidden to trade there. Rich beavers, otters, martins and foxes are found there. This cargo consists of five hundred otter skins, and fifteen hundred beavers, and a few other things, which were in four parcels, for twenty-eight thousand, some hundred guilders.*

This country, or the river Montagne, called by our's Mauritius, was first sailed to by the worthy Hendrick Christiaensen van Cleef. When he went a voyage to the West Indies, he happened near there. But his vessel being deeply laden, and a ship belonging to Monichendam having been wrecked in that neighbourhood, he durst not approach that land; this he postponed, being desirous to do so another time. It so happened that he and the worthy Adriaen Block, chartered a ship with the skipper Ryser, and accomplished his voyage thither, bringing back with him two sons of the principal sachems there. Though

---

* The cargo of the New Netherland, was sold in Amsterdam on 20th Dec. 1624.

very dull men, they were expert enough in knavery. Hudson, the famous English pilot, had been there also, to reach the south sea, but found no passage; as men will read in the Netherlands History, in the year 1612.

This aforesaid Hendrick Christiaensz, after he had dissolved partnership with Adriaen Block, made ten voyages thither, in virtue of a grant from the Lords States, who gave him that privilege for the first establishment of the place. On the expiration of that privilege, this country was granted to the West India company, to draw their profits thence; as has already been done, and shall still further increase from the products which are manifest there, whereof further detail will be given in the next, as much depends on success.

Good care having been taken by the directors of the West India company, in the spring to provide everything for the colony in Virginia, near the Maykans on the river Mauritius, by us called New Netherland, special attention was directed this month, (April,) to reinforce it, as follows:

As the country is well adapted for agriculture and the raising of every thing that is produced here, the aforesaid Lords resolved to take advantage of the circumstance, and to provide the place with many necessaries, through the Honble. Pieter Evertsen Hulst, who undertook to ship thither, at his risk, whatever was requisite, to wit; one hundred and three head of cattle; stallions, mares, steers and cows, for breeding and multiplying, besides all the hogs and sheep that might be thought expedient to send thither; and to distribute these in two ships of one hundred and forty lasts, in such a manner that they should be well foddered and attended to. Each animal had its own stall, with a floor of three feet of sand; fixed as comfortably as any stall here. Each animal had its respective servant who attended to it and knew its wants so as to preserve its health, together with all suitable forage, such as oats, hay and straw, &c. In addition to these, country people take with them all furniture proper for the dairy; all sorts of seed, ploughs and agricultural implements, so that nothing is wanting. What is most remarkable is, that nobody in the two ships can discover where the water is stowed for these cattle. As it was necessary to have another (ship) on that account, I

shall here add :—the above parties caused a deck
to be constructed on board. Beneath this were
stowed in each ship three hundred tons of fresh
water which was pumped up and thus distributed
among the cattle. On this deck lay the ballast
and thereupon stood the horses and steers, and
thus there was no waste. He added the third
ship so that, should the voyage continue longer,
nothing may be wanting to the success of the
expedition. In the eyes of the far seeing, the plan
of this colony, which lay right beside the Spanish
passage from the West Indies, was well laid.

In company with these, goes a fast sailing
vessel at the risk of the directors. In these aforesaid vessels also go six complete families with
some freemen, so that forty five new comers or
inhabitants are taken out, to remain there. The
natives of New Netherland are very well disposed
so long as no injury is done them. But if any
wrong be committed against them they think it
long till they be revenged and should any one
against whom they have a grudge, be peaceably
walking in the woods or going along in his sloop,
even after a lapse of time, they will slay him,
though they are sure it will cost them their lives
on the spot, so highly prized is vengeance among
them.

In our previous discourses, mention is made of New Netherland. Here is additional information: On further enquiry it is found, that they have a chief in time of war, named *Sacjama*, but above him is a greater *Sacjama* (pointing to Heaven) who rules the sun and moon. When they wage war against each other, they fortify their tribe or nation with palisades, serving them for a fort, and sally out the one against the other. They have a tree in the centre, on which they place sentinels to observe the enemy and discharge arrows. None are exempt in war, but the priests, and the women who carry their husband's arrows and food. The meat they eat consists of game and fish; but the bread is cakes baked fore-father's fashion, in the ashes; they almost all eat that in war. They are a wicked, bad people, very fierce in arms. Their dogs are small. When the Honble. Lambrecht van Twenhuyzen, once a skipper,* had given them a big dog, and it was presented to them on ship-board, they were very much afraid of it; calling it, also, a Sachem of dogs, being the biggest. The dog, tied with a rope on board, was very furious against them, they being clad like beasts with skins, for he thought they were game; but when they gave

---

* Traded as early as 1614, 1615, to this country, under a special charter. See O'Call. Hist. N. Netherland i. 74 et seq.

him some of their bread made of Indian corn,
which grows there, he learned to distinguish
them, that they were men.

There are oaks of very close grain; yea, harder
than any in this country, as thick as three or four
men. There is Red-wood which being burned,
smells very agreeably; when men sit by the fire
on benches made from it, the whole house is
perfumed by it. When they keep watch by night
against their enemies, then they place it in the
centre of their huts, to warm their feet by it; they
do not sit, then, up in a tree, but make a hole in
the roof, and keep watch there, to prevent attacks.

Poisonous plants have been found there, which
should be studied by those who have a fancy to
cultivate land. Hendrick Christiaensen carried
thither, by order of his employers, bucks, and
goats, also rabbits, but they were found poisoned
by the herbs. The Directors intend to send thither
this spring voyage, [1625] a quantity of hogs
which will be of great service to the colony; to
be followed by cows, with young calves.

Very large oysters, sea fish and river fish are
in such very great abundance there, that they
cannot be sold; and in rivers so deep, as to be
navigated upwards with large ships.

The two lads brought hither by Adriaen Block,
were named Orson and Valentine. This Orson
was a thoroughly wicked scamp, and on his return

to his own country was the cause of Hendrick
Christiaensen's death; but he was paid in like
coin. He got a bullet as his recompence.

Chastity appears, on further enquiry, to hold a
place among them, they being unwilling to cohabit
with ours, through fear of their husbands. But
those who are single, evince every friendly dispo-
sition. Further information is necessary. Whatever else is of value in the country, such as mines
and other ores shall by time and further exploration
be made known to us. Much profit is to be
expected from good management.

At the same time arrived a ship from New
Netherland, mostly with furs. As far as good
order is concerned, all goes well there. The
vessels with the cattle had not yet got there; the
crops which our Colonists had planted, looked
well, but there was no certain information thereof.
The next will bring their owners good news.

A ship came, at the same time, to the aforesaid
Company from New Germany, loaded mostly
with peltries, which had a favorable voyage. The
cattle carried thither, were removed upwards to a
convenient place abounding with grass and
pasture. Only two animals died on the passage.
This gave great satisfaction to the adventurers,
who had found the voyage so pleasant.

History of New Netherland,

1626-1630.

In our preceding Treatise we made mention of New Netherland and its colony planted by the West India Company, situate in Virginia on the river, called by the French Montaigne, and by us, Mauritius, and that some families were sent thither, which now increased to two hundred souls ; and afterwards some ships, one with horses, the other with cows, and the third hay; two months afterwards a fleet was equipped, carrying sheep, hogs, wagons, ploughs, and all other implements of husbandry.

These cattle were, on their arrival, first landed on Nut Island, three miles up the river, where they remained a day or two. There being no means of pasturing them there, they were shipped in sloops and boats to the Manhates, right opposite said Island. Being put out to pasture here, they throve well, but afterwards full twenty in all died. The cause of this was that they had eaten something bad from an uncultivated soil. But they went in the middle of September [1625] on new grass, as good and as long as could be desired.

The Colony was planted at this time, on the Manhates where a Fort was staked out by Master Kryn Frederycke an engineer. It will be of large dimensions. The ship which has returned home this month (Nov.)* brings samples of all the different sorts of produce there. The cargo consists of 7246 beavers, 675 otter skins, 48 minx, 36 wild cat, and various other sorts; several pieces of oak timber, and hickory.

The counting house there is kept in a stone building, thatched with reed: the other houses are of the bark of trees. Each has his own house. The Director and Koopman live together ; there are thirty ordinary houses on the east side of the river which runs nearly north and south. The Honble. Pieter Minuit is Director there at present ; Jan Lempo Schout [Sheriff] ; Sebastiaen Jansz Crol and Jan Huyck, comforters of the sick, who, whilst awaiting a clergyman, read to the commonalty there on Sundays, from texts of Scripture with the Comment. François Molemaecker is busy building a horse-mill, over which shall be constructed a spacious room sufficient to accommodate a large congregation, and then a tower is to be erected where the bells brought from Porto Rico will be hung.

The Council there administered justice in criminal

------

* The Arms of Amsterdam, sailed from the Manhattans on 23d Septr. 1626.

matters as far as imposing fines (*boet-straffe*), but not as far as capital punishment. Should it happen that any one deserves that, he must be sent to Holland with his sentence. Cornelis May of Hoorn was in the year 1624, the first director there; Willem Van Hulst was the second in the year 1625. He returns now. There is another there who fills no public office ; he is busy about his own affairs. Men work there as in Holland ; one trades upwards, southwards and northwards; another builds houses, the third farms. Each farmer has his farm and the cows on the land purchased by the Company; but the milk remains to the profit of the Boor ; he sells it to those of the people who receive their wages for work every week. The houses of the Hollanders now stand without the fort, but when that is completed, they will all repair within, so as to garrison it and be secure from sudden attack.

Those of the South River will abandon their Fort, and come hither ; no more than fifteen or sixteen men will remain at Fort Orange, the most distant point at which the Hollanders traded ; the remainder will come down to the Manhates. Right opposite is the fort of the Maykans which they built against their enemies the Maquaes [Mohawks] a powerful people.

It happened this year, that the Maykans, being at war with the Maquaes, requested to be assisted by the Commander of Fort Orange and six others. Commander Krieckebeck went up with them a mile from the Fort, and met the Maquaes who peppered them so bravely with a discharge of arrows, that they were forced to fly, leaving many slain among whom were the Commander and three of his men. Among the latter was Tymen Bouwensz., whom they devoured, after having well cooked him. The rest they burnt The Commander was buried with the other two by his side. Three escaped; two Portuguese and a Hollander from Hoorn. One of the Portuguese was wounded by an arrow in the back whilst swimming. The Indians carried a leg and an arm home to be divided among their families, as a proof that they had conquered their enemies.

Some days after the worthy Pieter Barentsen, who usually was sent upwards and along the coast with the sloops, visited them; they wished to excuse their act on the plea that they had never injured the whites and asked the reason why the latter had meddled with them; Had it been otherwise, they would not have acted as they had.

There being no Commander, Pieter Barentsen assumed the command of Fort Orange by order of Director Minuit. There were eight families there, and ten or twelve seamen in the Company's service. The fort was to remain garrisoned by sixteen men, with out women, and the families were to leave there this year in order to strenthen with people the colony near the Manhates who were becoming more and more accustomed to the strangers.

The natives are always seeking some advantage by thieving. The crime is seldom punished among them. If any one commit that offence too often he is stript bare of his goods, and must resort to other means another time. The husband who abandons his wife without cause must leave all her's; in like manner the wife the husband's. But as they love the children ardently, these are frequently the cause of their coming again together. The girls allow their hair to be cut all around, like the priests, when they are unwell for the first time. They work apart from all the men in a separate house, where food is furnished them on a stick. They remain therein until they are sick a second time. Then they make their appearance abroad again, and are allowed to marry. They then again dress their hair, which before they would not touch. The married women let their hair grow to the waist and smear it with oil. When they are unwell they do not eat with their husbands, and they sup the drink out of the hand. The men let the hair grow on one side of the head for a braid; the rest is cut off. If one kill the other, it is not punished; whoever it concerns meditates vengeance if satisfaction be not made. In the month of August a universal torment seizes them, so that they run like men possessed, regarding neither hedges nor ditches, and like mad dogs resting no where except from sheer inability. They hold this in singular respect. The birds most common are wild pigeons; these are so numerous that they shut out the sunshine.

When the fort, staked out at the Manhates, will be completed, it is to be named Amsterdam. The fort at the South River is already vacated, in order to strengthen the colony. For purposes of trade, only one yacht is sent there, in order to avoid expense.

The Sickenanes dwell about the north, between the Brownists and the Dutch. The chief of this nation hath lately made an agreement with Pieter Barents, not to trade with any other than him. Jaques Elekes had imprisoned him in the year 1622 in his yacht and obliged him to pay a heavy ransom, or else he should "cup" him. He paid one hundred and forty fathoms of zeewan, which consists of small beads they manufacture themselves, and which they prize as jewels. On this account he has no confidence in any one but Barentsen now.

The Brownists, who live beyond them, are Englishmen, who removed thither by consent of the King. They are called Puritans, because they seek after purity in the orthodox religion. They wished not to live in England; desiring not wealth, but merely necessaries and frugality.

The most distant nations from there, known to the traders, are the Indians from French Canada. Thereabout are the Orankokx, the Achkokx and others, both men and women. On entering the river, if they bring women with them, 'tis a sign they are friends; if they visit the yachts without these, every one must be on his guard.

The belief of the Maikans regarding the separation of the soul is, that it goes up westward on leaving the body. There 'tis met with great rejoicing by the others who died previously; there they wear black otter or bear skins, which among them are signs of gladness. They have no desire to be with them. The Mahieu, captain of the Maykans. who is named Cat, pretends that death is the offspring of the devil, who is evil. A skipper denying this, said, God had control over death. Thereupon he asked, if He being good had the power to give, or take away life? And he was answered, Yea; which he could not understand, how this good God should inflict evil, that is death. But there was no one to furnish him proper instruction; he therefore remains in his darkness. When they have a corpse, they place it, in the act of dying, squat on the heels, like children sitting in this country before the fire; and so lay it in the grave, all sitting; its face to the east.

It appears that the Sickanamers, before mentioned, make a sort of sacrifice. They have a hole in a hill in which they place a kettle full of all sorts of articles that they have, either by them, or procured. When there is a great quantity collected a snake comes in, then they all depart, and the Manittou, that is the devil, comes in the night and takes the kettle away, according to the statement of the Koutsinacka, or devil hunter, who presides over the ceremony.

This Pieter Barentz, already spoken of, is conversant with all the tribes thereabout ; he traded with the Sickenames, to whom the whole north coast is tributary ; with the Sinnekox, Wappenox, Maquaes and Maikans, so that he visited all the tribes with sloops and traded in a friendly manner with them, only for peltries. And he brought back this year a valuable cargo in the ship the Arms of Amsterdam, whereof Adriaen Joris is skipper, who went out there on the 19th of December of the year 1625 with the Sea-gull (*het Meeutje*) and conveyed Pieter Minuit aforesaid, who now sends for his wife thither. The Sea gull arrived there 4th May, 1626.

Two ships came from New Netherland for the benefit of the said (W. I.) Company, with ten thousand peltries, or skins, together with a large quantity of timber fit for the building of the vessels which are shortly to be launched. Those ships were despatched by the Commander there, called Minuict ; one ship was the Three Kings, skipper Jan Jacobsz of Wieringh ;* the other was, the Arms of Amsterdam.

The government over the people of New Netherland continued on the 19th of August of this year in the aforesaid Minuict, successor to Verhulst, who went thither from Holland on 9th January, Anno, 1626, and took up his residence in the midst of a nation called Manhates, building a fort there, to be called

---

* Sent in 1627 from the Dutch as delegate to New Plymouth.

Amsterdam, having four points and faced outside entirely with stone, as the walls of sand fall down, and are now more compact. The population consists of two hundred and seventy souls, including men, women, and children. They remained as yet without the Fort, in no fear, as the natives live peaceably with them. They are situate three miles from the Sea, on the river by us called Mauritius, by others, Rio de Montagne.

These strangers for the most part occupy their farms. Whatever they require is supplied by the Directors. The winter grain has turned out well there, but the summer grain which ripened before it was half grown in consequence of the excessive heat, was very light. The cattle sent thither have had a good increase, and every thing promises better, as soon as the land is improved, which is very poor and scrubby.

There are now no families at Fort Orange, situated higher up the river among the Maikans. They are all brought down. They keep five or six and twenty persons, traders, there. Bastiaen Janz Crol is Vice Director there; he remained there since the year 1626, when the others came down.

Those of the West India Company have removed all those who were at the South River. Only one trading vessel is kept there. Traders who come from a great distance make mention of lion skins which will not be bartered, because they are used for clothing, being much warmer than others.

Beyond the South River, in 37 degrees, English-men are settled, freemen, but planted there by merchants on condition, that they deliver as much tobacco to their masters as is agreed on ; the remainder is their own. Considerable trade was carried on with them, and many ships come thither from England.

On the north side are the English Brownists, who maintain themselves very well and acquire consider-able strength, supporting their reputation bravely with the natives, whom they do not fear, having acted strictly with these from the first, and so continuing.

In the beginning of this year, war broke out between the Maikans near Fort Orange and the Makwaes, but these beat and captured the Maikans, and drove off the remainder who have settled towards the north by the Fresh River so called ;* where they begin again to cultivate the soil; and thus the war terminated.

After the Right Honble Lords Directors of the Privileged West India Company in the United Netherlands, had provided for the defence of New Netherland and put everything there in good order, they taking into consideration the advantages of said place, the favorable nature of the air, and soil, and that considerable trade and goods and many com-modities may be obtained from thence, sent some persons, of their own accord, thither with all sorts of cattle and implements necessary for agriculture, so

---

* Connecticut River.

that in the year 1628 there already resided on the
island of the Manhattes, two hundred and seventy
souls, men, women, and children, under Governor
Minuit, Verhulst's successor, living there in peace
with the natives. But as the land, in many p'aces
being full of weeds and wild productions, could not
be properly cultivated in consequence of the scanti-
ness of the population, the said Lords Directors of the
West India Company, the better to people their lands,
& to bring the country to produce more abundantly,
resolved to grant divers privileges, freedoms, and
exemptions to all patroons, masters or individuals who
should plant any colonies and cattle in New Netherland, and they accordingly have constituted and
published in print (certain) exemptions, to afford better
encouragement and infuse greater zeal into whomso-
ever should be inclined to reside and plant his colonie
in New Netherland.

FINIS.

APPENDICES.

———◦⟨◆⟩◦———

APPENDIX I.

EARLY DUTCH SETTLEMENT ON THE DELAWARE.

(Deed Book, VII.)

N. York, february 14: 1684-5.

The Deposicon of Catelina Trico aged fouer score yeares or thereabouts taken before the right honoble. Collo. Thomas Dongan Lieut. and Governour under his Royll. highss James Duke of Yorke and Albany etc. of N York and its dependencyes in America, who saith and Declares in the prsens of God as followeth

That she Came to this Province either in the yeare one thousand six hundred and twenty three or twenty fouer to the best of her remembrance, and that fouer Women Came along with her in the same Shipp, in which ship the Governor Arian Jorissen Came also over, which fouer Women were married at Sea and that they and their husbandes stayed about three Weekes at this place and then they with eight seamen more went in a vessell by ordr. of the Dutch Gover-

no_r. to Dellaware River and there settled. This I
Certifie under my hand and y^e seale of this province.

THO. DONGAN.

The Deposicon of Arien Dirksen Korn aged about
sixty five yeares being Deposed saith

That he Came in this Country of New York
formerly called the new Netherlands in the yeare one
thousand six hundd. and thirty the 24th of May with
the ship Vnity John Brower Commander and hath
ever since eontinued here in this country, and saith
further that att the said time of his arrivall here this
Deponent heard and was Informed by persons then
arriving here from Delleware River that the said
River was settled by the dutch west India Company,
who had sent a parcell of men there in order to whale
fishing, and this Deponent saith further that some
short time After to his best Remembrance it was
about one yeare or one yeare and a half after news
Came here att New York from Deleware, that all
the said people in Delleware were Cutt of by the
Indians, and further this Deponent saith nott.

Deposed by the said Aron Dirksen Korn Coram
me the 16th. March 1684-5.

Peter Lawrrsen aged sixty seaven yeares being
deposed saith that he came into this Province a
servant to t^h west india Company in the yeare 1628

and in the yeare 1630 by order of the West india
Company hee with seven more were sent in a sloope
with hoy sayle to dellaware where the Company had
a trading house with ten or twelve servants belonging
to it which the deponant himselfe did see there
settled, and he further saith that at his returne from
Delaware River the said vessell stopt at the hoorekill
where the Deponant did alsoe see a settlemᵗ. of a
brickhouse belonging to the west India Company, and
the Deponant further saith that upon an Island neare
the falls of that River and neare the west side thereof
the said Company some three or fouer yeares afore had a
trading house where there were three or foure familyes
of Walloons the place of there settlemᵗ. he saw and
that they had been seated there he was Informed by
some of the said Walloons themselves When they
were returned from thence and further this Deponent
saith not.

 This Deposicon was taken upon oath before me
which I doe Certifie under the seale of this Province
this 24th of March Aᵒ. 1684-5 in New Yorke.

T. D.

APPENDIX II.

THE FIRST WHITE WOMAN IN ALBANY.

(N. Y. Col: MSS. XXXV.)

CATELYN TRICO aged about 83 years born in Paris
doth Testify and Declare that in yᶜ year 1623 she
came into this Country w ʰ a Ship called yᶜ Unity
whereof was Commander Arien Jorise belonging to
yᶜ West India Company being yᶜ first Ship yᵗ came
here for yᶜ sᵈ Company ; as soon as they came to
Mannatans now called N: York they sent Two
families & six men to harford River & Two families
& 8 men to Delaware River and 8 men they left att
N: Yorke to take Possession and yᵉ Rest of yᶜ Pas-
sengers went wᵗʰ yᶜ Ship up as farr as Albany which
they then Called fort Orangie When as yᶜ Ship came
as farr as Sopus which is ½ way to Albanie ; they
lightned yᶜ Ship wᵗʰ some boats yᵗ were left there by
yᶜ Dutch that had been there yᶜ year before a trade-
ing wᵗʰ yᶜ Indians upont there oune accompts & gone
back again to Holland & so brought yᶜ vessel up ;
there were about 18 families aboard who settled themselves att Albany and made a small fort ; and as
soon as they had built themselves some hutts of
Bark : yᶜ Mahikanders or River Indians. yᶜ Maquase:
Oneydes : Onnondages Cayougas. & Sinnekes, wᵗʰ

y^c Mahawawa or Ottawawaes Indians came & made
Covenants of friendship wth ye s^d Arien Jorise there
Commander Bringing him great Presents of Bever
o^r oy^r Peltry and desyred that they might come &
have a Constant free Trade with them wch was con-
cluded upon & y^c s^d nations came dayly with great
multidus of Bever and traded them wth ye Christians,
there s^d Commanr Arien Jorise staid with them all
winter and sent his sonne home with y^c ship;
ye s^d Deponent lived in Albany three years all which
time y^c s^d Indians were all as quiet as Lambs & came
& Traded with all ye freedom Imaginable, in y^c year
1626 ye Deponent came from Albany & settled at
N: Yorke where she lived afterwards for many years
and then came to Long Island where she now lives.

The s^d Catelyn Trico made oath of y^c s^d Deposi-
tion before me at her house on Long Island in
ye Wale Bought this 17th day of October 1688.

WILLIAM MORRIS

Justice of y^e pece

THE END.

www.ingramcontent.com/pod-product-compliance
Lightning Source LLC
Chambersburg PA
CBHW031450270326
41930CB00007B/936